girlfriends are lifesavers

Reeda Joseph

VIVA
EDITIONS

Published in the United States by Viva Editions, an imprint of Cleis Press Inc., P.O. Box 14697, San Francisco, California 94114.

Printed in Hong Kong.
Cover design: Michele Wetherbee
Interior design: Michele Wetherbee and Madeleine Budnick
10 9 8 7 6 5 4 3 2 1

Library of Congress Cataloging-in-Publication Data

Joseph, Reeda.
Girlfriends are lifesavers / Reeda Joseph. -- 1st ed.
    p. cm.
ISBN 978-1-57344-359-3 (alk. paper)
1. Friendship--Humor. 2. Female friendship--Humor. I. Title.
PN6231.F748J67 2009
818'.602--dc22

                        2009022457

dear reader,

Husbands and boyfriends are nice accessories, but girlfriends are the essential must-haves of life. It's our gal pals who get us through both good times and bad. The course of my life has been charted over coffee with the girls, new plans made over a margarita (or two), and many a late-night phone call dedicated to the topic of love. Who else do we turn to for the best advice, gossip, and fashion tips? Featuring a treasury of vintage vixens from my collection, each page of **Girlfriends Are Life-savers** celebrates a different aspect of friendship—from sharing secrets to sharing tears, from being each other's cheerleaders to comforting one another with hugs and good advice. Filled with love, laughter, and heartfelt caring, **Girlfriends Are Lifesavers** honors everything it means to be a true friend.

As someone once said, "Friendship isn't a big thing, it's a million little things." This book of women's wisdom is a tribute to these sisters of the soul who are there every step of the way. If you've ever told a girlfriend "Love you like a sister!," this book is for you.

Your friend,

reeda

"This confection of a book is like candy—tart, satisfying, and so much sweeter when it's shared. A cheeky homage to the unbreakable bonds between women."

—Ame Mahler Beanland and Emily Miles Terry, authors of the *New York Times* bestsellers **Nesting: It's a ChickThing** and **It's a Chick Thing: Celebrating the Wild Side of Women's Friendships**

Best friends

are what make

the good old

days so *good.*

Our **friendship** has taught me more than any book could.

We can be ourselves with
our closest friends...

baggage and all.

If they only knew what we really talk about at coffee with the girls…

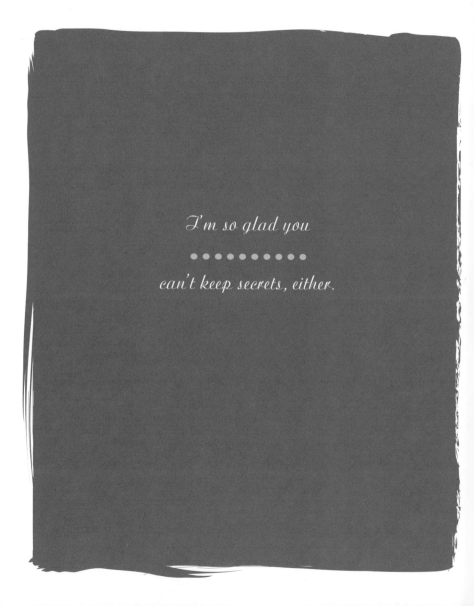

I'm so glad you

● ● ● ● ● ● ● ● ● ● ●

can't keep secrets, either.

We rely on
our girlfriends
for so many
important
things…like
gossip, dirt,
and rumors.

...remember everything...

even things
I wish you
would forget.

You and I are neither
sweet nor innocent (but
they don't know that).

Sometimes we have to act
excited for each other, even
when we wish someone had
sent us the *damn flowers.*

We've gotten

through some

pretty tough

times together,

like *bathing suit*

season!

Rain or
shine...

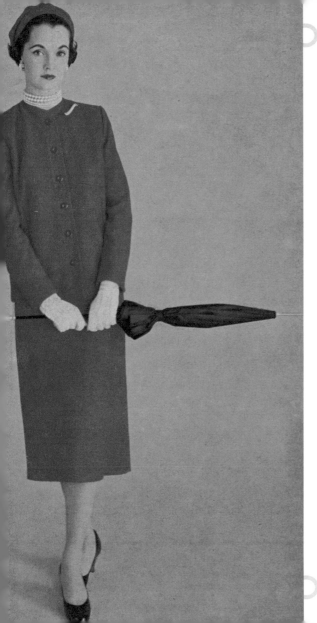

we've got each
other's back!

Should we have had that third round

The Amer

Dream...

...compliments
of Prozac.

They might
not admit it,
but even the
best of friends
have a little
competition
going on.

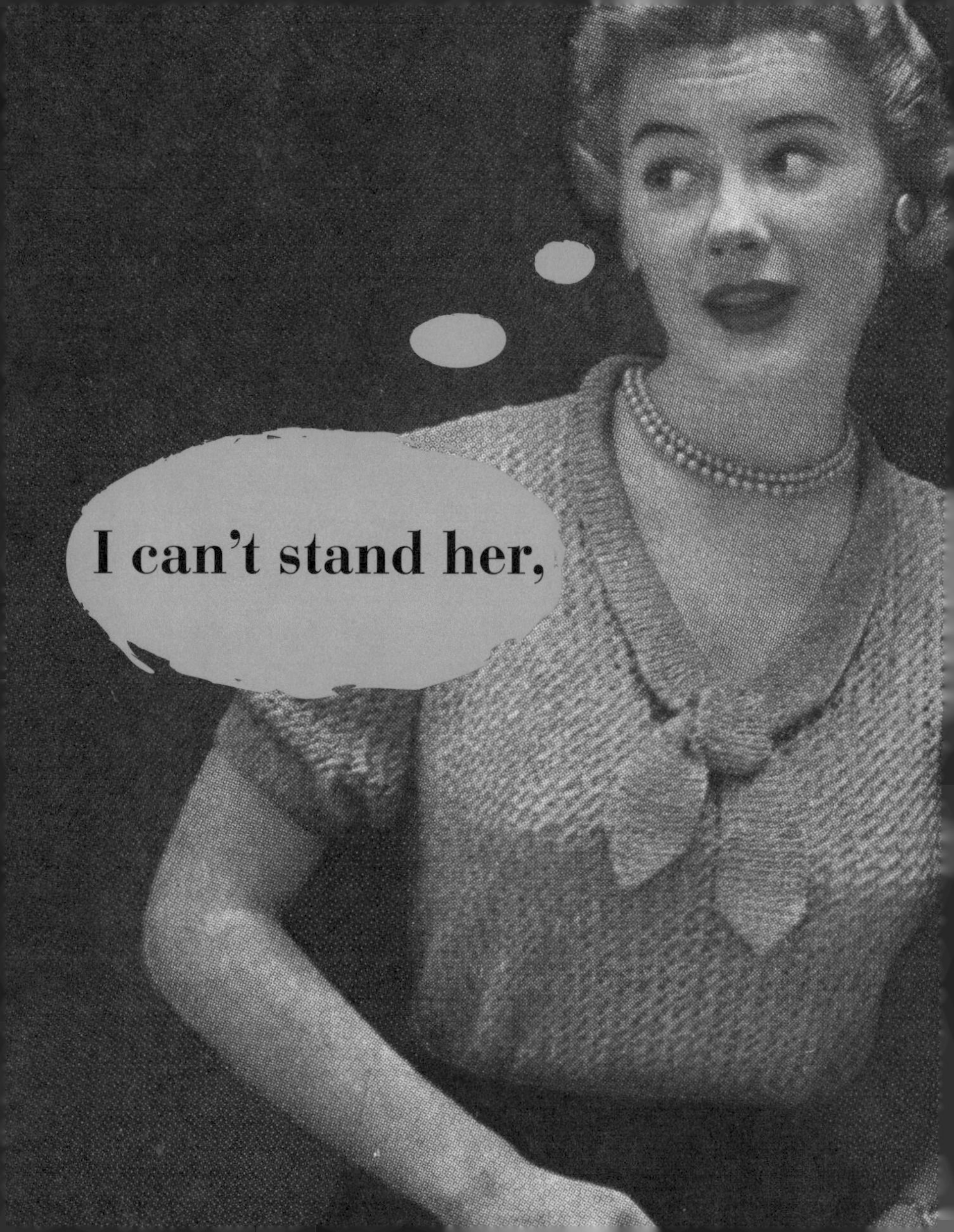
I can’t stand her,

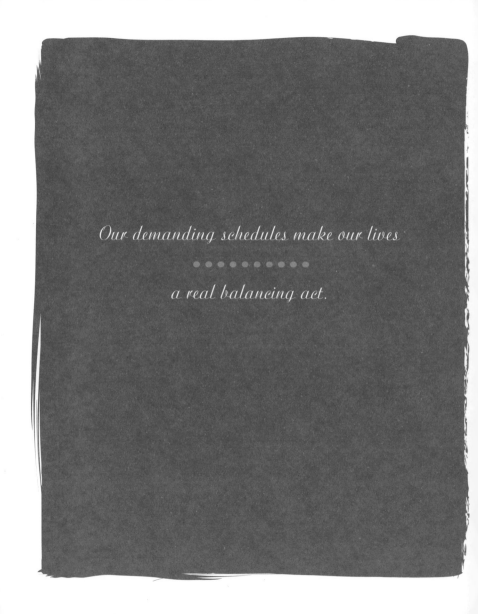

Our demanding schedules make our lives

• • • • • • • • • •

a real balancing act.

What

happens

in Boise

stays in…

Boise.

If you don't have

nything good to say...

about
anybody,
come sit
by me.

How do you like my
Halloween costume?

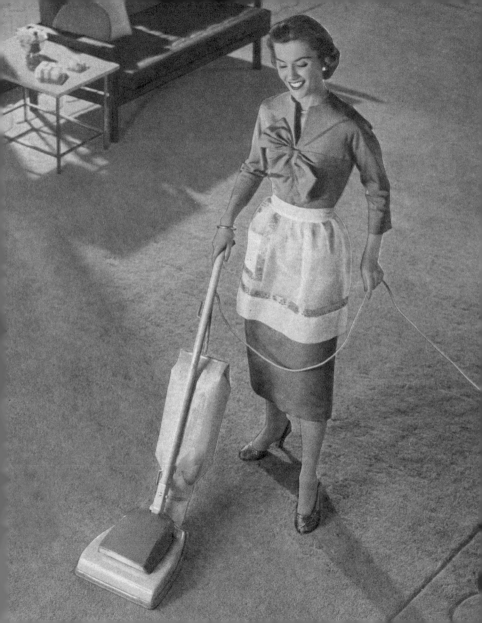

Bette Davis

was right:

getting old

is not for

wimps!

We can admit it…we like labels.
Prada, Chanel, or Princess suit us just fine.

girlfriends

put up with each other

even through all our **moods.**

The trick is to not let men
know that we're smarter.

Friendship

is one fashion

that will never

go out of *style.*

It seemed like a good idea
at the time…

You take the surfer

and I'll take the lifeguard.

Hmmm,

he didn't look

so gay on

Facebook!

Our favorite form of therapy...

● ● ● ● ● ● ● ● ● ● ●

SHOPPING!

But do you even **rememb**er

your natural shade?

Everything gets better...

when you
can vent
about it
with your
girlfriends.

reeda joseph has been a collector of one-of-a-kind nostalgic items since childhood. From church basements to garage sales to the flea markets of Paris, Reeda is constantly searching for (and finding) vintage images. A designer of cards and stationery for WrightCardCo.com, she lives in San Francisco, California.